The Science of Taste Exploring Food and Beverage Engineering

AYN RAND

The Science of Taste Exploring Food and Beverage Engineering

Copyright © 2023 by AYN RAND

All rights reserved. No part of this book may be reproduced or transmitted in any form or by any means, electronic or mechanical, including photocopying, recording, or by any information storage and retrieval system, without permission in writing from the publisher.

This book is a work of fiction. Names, characters, places, and incidents either are the product of the author's imagination or are used fictitiously. Any resemblance to actual events, locales, persons, living or dead, is entirely coincidental.

The first edition was published in 2023

ISBN:
Published by:
Sunshine
1663 Liberty Drive
Hyderabad, IN 47403
www.Sunshinepublishers.com

This book is self-published using on-demand printing and publishing, which allows it to be printed and distributed globally

TABLE OF CONTENT

Chapter 1: Introduction to Food and Beverage Engineering   07

The Importance of Taste in Food and Beverage Engineering

History and Evolution of Food and Beverage Engineering

Current Trends and Challenges in the Field

Chapter 2: Understanding the Science of Taste   13

The Five Basic Tastes: Sweet, Sour, Salty, Bitter, and Umami

The Role of Taste Receptors and the Brain in Taste Perception

Factors Influencing Taste Perception: Genetics, Age, and Culture

Chapter 3: Principles of Food and Beverage Engineering 19

Food and Beverage Formulation: Balancing Taste and Nutritional Value

Techniques for Enhancing Flavor Profiles

The Role of Texture in Taste Perception

Chapter 4: Food and Beverage Processing Techniques 25

Preservation Techniques: Canning, Freezing, and Drying

Fermentation and its Impact on Taste

Food and Beverage Packaging: Ensuring Taste and Quality

Chapter 5: Innovations in Food and Beverage Engineering 31

Molecular Gastronomy: The Science behind Culinary Creations

Sensory Analysis: Evaluating Taste and Quality

Food and Beverage Product Development: From Concept to Market

Chapter 6: The Future of Food and Beverage Engineering 37

Sustainable Food and Beverage Production

Advances in Food and Beverage Manufacturing Technologies

Exploring Novel Ingredients and Flavors

Chapter 7: Applications of Food and Beverage Engineering in Various Industries 43

Food and Beverage Engineering in the Restaurant Industry

Food and Beverage Engineering in the Pharmaceutical Industry

Food and Beverage Engineering in the Beverage Manufacturing Industry

Chapter 8: Case Studies and Success Stories 50

Innovations in Food and Beverage Engineering: Case Studies of Successful Products

Interviews with Food and Beverage Engineers: Their Journey and Contributions

Chapter 9: Ethical Considerations in Food and Beverage Engineering 54

Ensuring Food Safety and Quality

Addressing Health Concerns and Nutritional Challenges

Sustainable and Ethical Sourcing of Ingredients

Chapter 10: Conclusion and Future Outlook 60

Recapitulating the Science of Taste in Food and Beverage Engineering

Potential Future Developments in the Field

Inspiring the Next Generation of Food and Beverage Engineers

Chapter 1: Introduction to Food and Beverage Engineering

The Importance of Taste in Food and Beverage Engineering

Introduction:
Food and beverage engineering is a fascinating field that combines the principles of chemical engineering with the art of creating delicious and appealing products. While many aspects of this discipline are crucial, taste stands out as one of the most significant factors in determining the success of a food or drink. In this subchapter, we will explore the importance of taste in food and beverage engineering and its relevance to the field of chemical engineering.

Taste as a Sensory Experience:
Taste is a complex sensory experience that involves not only the taste buds on our tongues but also our sense of smell, texture, and even visual perception. It is the combination of these factors that determines how we perceive the flavors of food and beverages. Food and beverage engineers must understand the intricate interplay between these sensory elements to create products that are not only delicious but also visually appealing and satisfying to the palate.

Consumer Preferences and Market Demand:
The taste of a product plays a crucial role in consumer preferences and market demand. People are naturally drawn to foods and beverages that taste good and offer a pleasurable experience. Food and beverage engineers must consider the target audience and their preferences when formulating recipes and creating new products. By understanding the flavor profiles that appeal to different

niches, chemical engineers can develop innovative and tasty products that cater to specific consumer needs.

Balancing Taste with Health and Nutrition:
In today's health-conscious world, taste must be balanced with health and nutrition. Food and beverage engineers face the challenge of creating products that not only taste great but also meet nutritional requirements and dietary restrictions. This involves careful formulation and the use of alternative ingredients to reduce sugar, salt, and unhealthy fats without compromising on taste. Chemical engineers play a vital role in developing innovative techniques and processes to achieve this delicate balance.

Quality Control and Product Consistency:
Taste is also critical in quality control and ensuring product consistency. Food and beverage engineers must develop reliable methods to measure taste objectively and maintain consistency across batches. This involves sensory testing, flavor analysis, and the use of advanced technology to detect any deviations in taste. By monitoring taste throughout the production process, chemical engineers can guarantee that the final products meet the desired flavor profiles consistently.

Conclusion:
The importance of taste in food and beverage engineering cannot be overstated. From creating delightful sensory experiences to meeting consumer preferences, taste plays a significant role in the success of food and beverage products. Chemical engineers in this field have the unique opportunity to combine their knowledge of chemistry and engineering principles with the art of creating delicious and appealing flavors. By understanding the importance of taste, these professionals can innovate and develop products that not only satisfy the palate but also meet the demands of a diverse and health-conscious market.

History and Evolution of Food and Beverage Engineering

Food and beverage engineering is a fascinating field that combines the principles of chemical engineering with the art of crafting delicious and nutritious food and beverages. In this subchapter, we will explore the history and evolution of this field, from its humble beginnings to the modern advancements that have shaped the way we produce and consume food and drinks.

The origins of food and beverage engineering can be traced back to ancient civilizations, where people developed various methods to preserve and process food. Techniques such as fermentation, drying, and smoking were used to extend the shelf life of perishable foods and enhance their flavors. These early innovations laid the foundation for the field of food engineering, albeit in a rudimentary form.

Fast forward to the Industrial Revolution in the 18th century, and we see significant advancements in food and beverage engineering. The invention of steam-powered machinery revolutionized food processing, allowing for mass production and improved efficiency. Canning and pasteurization techniques were also developed during this time, further enhancing food safety and preservation.

As the understanding of chemistry and microbiology grew, so did the field of food and beverage engineering. In the early 20th century, breakthroughs such as the discovery of vitamins and the development of synthetic food additives paved the way for the creation of more nutritious and flavorful foods. This period also saw the rise of large-scale food processing plants, which utilized various engineering principles to increase productivity and meet the growing demands of a rapidly expanding population.

In recent decades, food and beverage engineering has become even more sophisticated, thanks to advancements in technology and research. Techniques such as freeze-drying, high-pressure processing, and molecular gastronomy have emerged, allowing for the creation of innovative food products and culinary experiences. Additionally, the field has focused on sustainability and reducing waste, with engineers developing new methods for food packaging, storage, and distribution.

Today, food and beverage engineering plays a crucial role in ensuring the safety, quality, and sustainability of the food we consume. Chemical engineers work tirelessly to optimize production processes, improve nutritional value, and develop new methods for food preservation. They also collaborate with other disciplines such as biology, physics, and materials science to push the boundaries of innovation in the food and beverage industry.

In conclusion, the history and evolution of food and beverage engineering have been shaped by centuries of ingenuity and scientific advancements. From ancient preservation techniques to modern-day technological innovations, this field continues to evolve, providing us with a diverse array of delicious and nutritious food and beverages. Whether you are a student of chemical engineering or simply interested in the science of taste, exploring the history of food and beverage engineering offers valuable insights into the intersection of science, technology, and culinary art.

Current Trends and Challenges in the Field

In the fast-paced world of food and beverage engineering, staying up-to-date with the latest trends and overcoming challenges is crucial. As chemical engineers, it is essential to understand the current landscape and be prepared for the ever-evolving demands of this industry. In this subchapter, we delve into the trends and challenges that are shaping the field of food and beverage engineering.

One prominent trend in recent years is the growing demand for healthier and more sustainable food and beverage options. Consumers are increasingly conscious of their dietary choices and the impact of their consumption on the environment. Chemical engineers play a vital role in developing innovative processes and ingredients that cater to these preferences. From plant-based proteins to natural sweeteners, the field is witnessing a shift towards more sustainable and nutritious alternatives.

Another emerging trend is the integration of technology and artificial intelligence (AI) in food and beverage engineering. The use of advanced sensors, data analytics, and automation is revolutionizing the industry. Chemical engineers are leveraging these technologies to optimize production processes, monitor quality control, and enhance product development. From precision farming to smart packaging solutions, technology is reshaping the way we produce, distribute, and consume food and beverages.

However, along with these trends come unique challenges. One of the primary challenges faced by chemical engineers in this field is ensuring food safety. With a globalized supply chain, it is crucial to prevent contamination and maintain the highest standards of hygiene throughout the production process. Chemical engineers are constantly developing new methodologies and technologies to mitigate risks and ensure the safety of the food and beverages we consume.

Additionally, the field also faces challenges related to waste management and resource optimization. As the population continues to grow, food waste and water scarcity have become critical issues. Chemical engineers are working towards developing sustainable solutions to reduce waste, enhance recycling processes, and optimize water usage in the food and beverage industry.

In conclusion, the field of food and beverage engineering is witnessing exciting trends and challenges. From the demand for healthier and sustainable options to the integration of technology and AI, the industry is evolving rapidly. Chemical engineers play a pivotal role in shaping this landscape, developing innovative processes and solutions to meet the changing needs of consumers. However, challenges such as ensuring food safety and optimizing resource usage need to be addressed. By staying informed, embracing innovation, and collaborating across disciplines, chemical engineers can continue to drive the advancements in the science of taste and contribute to a more sustainable and delicious future for all.

Chapter 2: Understanding the Science of Taste

The Five Basic Tastes: Sweet, Sour, Salty, Bitter, and Umami

Taste is an essential aspect of our daily lives. It not only helps us determine the deliciousness of our meals, but it also plays a significant role in our overall health and well-being. In this subchapter, we will explore the five basic tastes: sweet, sour, salty, bitter, and umami, and delve into the fascinating world of taste from a chemical engineering perspective.

Sweetness is perhaps the most universally loved taste. It is associated with sugars and is often found in fruits, desserts, and candies. From a chemical engineering standpoint, the sensation of sweetness is triggered by the presence of certain molecules, such as glucose and fructose, which interact with specific taste receptors on our tongues.

On the other end of the spectrum, we have bitterness. Bitterness is often associated with substances like coffee, dark chocolate, and certain vegetables. Chemical engineers study the compounds responsible for bitterness, such as alkaloids and flavonoids, to understand how they interact with taste receptors and how to mitigate or enhance their effects.

Sourness, as the name suggests, is the taste associated with acidity. It can be found in citrus fruits, vinegar, and fermented foods. Chemical engineers analyze the pH levels and the concentration of acids in various food and beverage products to ensure the desired level of sourness is achieved.

Saltiness is a taste that is easily recognizable and widely used in cooking. Sodium chloride, or table salt, is the primary compound responsible for this taste. Chemical engineers play a crucial role in determining the optimal amount of salt needed in food products, as excessive salt intake can lead to health issues such as hypertension.

Lastly, we have umami, a taste that is often described as savory or meaty. Umami is found in foods like tomatoes, mushrooms, and aged cheeses. The chemical compound responsible for this taste is glutamate, which stimulates specific taste receptors and enhances the overall flavor experience.

Understanding the five basic tastes is not only important for culinary purposes but also for the development of healthier and tastier food and beverage products. By studying the chemical interactions behind these tastes, chemical engineers can create innovative solutions to enhance flavor, reduce unhealthy additives, and cater to specific dietary needs.

In conclusion, the five basic tastes – sweet, sour, salty, bitter, and umami – are fundamental to our enjoyment and understanding of food. Chemical engineers play a vital role in unraveling the complexities of taste and using this knowledge to improve our culinary experiences, making food not just a necessity but a true delight for everyone.

The Role of Taste Receptors and the Brain in Taste Perception

Taste is an essential aspect of our daily lives that brings pleasure, nourishment, and cultural significance. Whether we savor a mouthwatering piece of chocolate or cringe at the bitterness of medicine, our sense of taste plays a crucial role in shaping our food preferences and overall well-being. But have you ever wondered how our taste buds transmit signals to our brain, enabling us to perceive different flavors? In this subchapter, we will delve into the fascinating world of taste receptors and the brain's role in taste perception.

Taste receptors are specialized cells found in taste buds located on the tongue, roof of the mouth, and throat. These receptors are responsible for detecting and transmitting information about the taste of food and beverages to our brain. Interestingly, taste receptors are not limited to a single type but are rather categorized into five main groups: sweet, salty, sour, bitter, and umami (the taste of savory and meaty flavors).

When we consume food, molecules from the food interact with the taste receptors on our taste buds. These interactions trigger a cascade of events that ultimately result in the transmission of signals to the brain. Each taste receptor group is designed to recognize specific molecules or chemical compounds associated with a particular taste. For example, sweet taste receptors detect sugars and artificial sweeteners, while bitter taste receptors respond to alkaloids, which are often found in toxic substances.

Once taste receptors are stimulated, they activate sensory neurons that send signals to the brain through the nervous system. The signals are then processed by various regions of the brain, including the gustatory cortex, which is responsible for taste perception. Remarkably, our brain combines taste information with other sensory inputs, such as smell and texture, to form a comprehensive perception of flavor.

Understanding the intricate relationship between taste receptors and the brain is not only fascinating but also has significant implications for the field of chemical engineering. Researchers and engineers can utilize this knowledge to develop innovative food and beverage products that cater to specific taste preferences. By manipulating taste receptors or enhancing certain flavors, they can create healthier alternatives or improve the overall sensory experience of existing products.

In conclusion, taste receptors and the brain work in harmony to allow us to experience the vast array of flavors in the world. By unraveling the complexities of taste perception, we gain a deeper appreciation for the role of chemical engineering in shaping our culinary experiences. So, the next time you indulge in your favorite dish, take a moment to appreciate the intricate dance happening between your taste buds and your brain.

Factors Influencing Taste Perception: Genetics, Age, and Culture

Taste perception is a complex phenomenon that is influenced by a variety of factors. In this subchapter, we will explore three key factors that play a significant role in shaping our individual taste preferences: genetics, age, and culture. Understanding these factors is crucial for both scientists and individuals seeking to explore the fascinating world of taste.

Genetics is one of the primary factors that contribute to our taste perception. Each individual has a unique genetic makeup that influences how they perceive different flavors. Genetic variations in taste receptors can determine whether someone is a "supertaster" - highly sensitive to certain tastes, or a "non-taster" - less sensitive to flavors. These variations can affect preferences for sweet, bitter, salty, or sour tastes. By studying genetic factors, scientists can gain valuable insights into why some individuals prefer certain foods over others.

Age is another influential factor in our taste perception. As we age, our taste buds naturally start to decline in sensitivity. This can lead to a decreased ability to detect subtle flavors and a preference for stronger, more intense tastes. Additionally, studies have shown that children often have a higher preference for sweet flavors, while adults tend to appreciate more complex and bitter tastes. Understanding the changes in taste perception throughout the lifespan can help researchers develop strategies to optimize the sensory experience of food and beverages for different age groups.

Culture plays a significant role in shaping our taste preferences. The foods we grow up eating and the culinary traditions of our culture heavily influence our taste perception. For example, in some cultures, spicy foods are a staple, and individuals develop a higher tolerance for heat. In contrast, other cultures may have a preference for milder flavors. Cultural experiences also shape our expectations and associations with certain tastes, further impacting our perception of flavors.

In conclusion, taste perception is a multi-faceted phenomenon influenced by genetics, age, and culture. Genetic variations in taste receptors determine our sensitivity to different flavors, while age-related changes and cultural experiences shape our preferences. Understanding these factors is crucial for scientists in the field of food and beverage engineering, as well as for individuals seeking to explore and appreciate the diverse world of taste. By unraveling the intricacies of taste perception, we can enhance the culinary experience for people from all walks of life.

Chapter 3: Principles of Food and Beverage Engineering

Food and Beverage Formulation: Balancing Taste and Nutritional Value

Food and beverage formulation is a critical aspect of the food industry that aims to strike a delicate balance between taste and nutritional value. In this subchapter, we will explore the intricacies of this process and delve into the role of chemical engineering in achieving the desired outcomes.

When it comes to food and beverage products, taste is undoubtedly the primary factor that influences consumer preference. However, the increasing awareness of the importance of a healthy diet has led to a growing demand for products that offer both great taste and nutritional value. This presents a challenge for food scientists and engineers who must find innovative ways to create products that satisfy the taste buds while also meeting the nutritional needs of consumers.

Chemical engineering plays a pivotal role in this process by utilizing scientific principles and engineering techniques to develop food and beverage formulations that are both delicious and nutritious. By understanding the chemical composition of various ingredients and their interactions, engineers can manipulate and optimize the formulation to achieve the desired sensory experience.

One crucial aspect of food and beverage formulation is the reduction of certain undesirable components such as salt, sugar, and unhealthy fats. Chemical engineers can employ their expertise to find alternative ingredients or utilize advanced techniques to lower the levels of these components without compromising taste. This may involve the use of flavor enhancers, natural sweeteners, or fat substitutes that can mimic the sensory attributes of the original ingredients.

Furthermore, chemical engineers can also focus on fortifying food and beverage products with essential nutrients, vitamins, and minerals. By utilizing their knowledge of ingredient interactions and processing techniques, they can ensure that these added nutritional elements are effectively incorporated into the formulation without negatively impacting the taste.

Ultimately, the goal of food and beverage formulation is to create products that cater to the diverse preferences and dietary needs of consumers. By combining the principles of taste and nutrition, chemical engineers can develop innovative formulations that strike the delicate balance between flavor and health. This subchapter serves as a valuable resource for anyone interested in understanding the science behind creating delicious and nutritious food and beverage products. Whether you are a food industry professional, a student of chemical engineering, or simply a curious individual, this exploration of food and beverage engineering will provide you with insights into the intricate process of formulating products that delight the taste buds while promoting a healthy lifestyle.

Techniques for Enhancing Flavor Profiles

In the world of food and beverage engineering, the science of taste plays a pivotal role in creating memorable culinary experiences. Understanding the intricacies of flavor profiles and the techniques to enhance them is essential for any aspiring chemical engineer or food enthusiast.

1. Extracting Natural Flavors: One technique to enhance flavor profiles is through the extraction of natural flavors. Chemical engineers employ various methods, such as distillation, infusion, or solvent extraction, to isolate and concentrate the aromatic compounds found in ingredients like herbs, spices, fruits, or vegetables. These extracted flavors can then be used to elevate the taste of a dish or beverage.

2. Fermentation: Fermentation is another technique that chemical engineers employ to enhance flavor profiles. By harnessing the power of microorganisms, such as yeast or bacteria, fermentation transforms the chemical composition of ingredients, resulting in complex and unique flavors. From traditional fermented foods like cheese, yogurt, or soy sauce to modern creations like craft beers or kombucha, fermentation is a versatile tool for flavor enhancement.

3. Molecular Gastronomy: Advances in food engineering have given rise to the field of molecular gastronomy, which explores the science behind the transformation of ingredients and the creation of novel flavor profiles. Chemical engineers employ techniques like spherification, foam creation, or culinary foams to manipulate textures, temperatures, and tastes, resulting in innovative culinary experiences.

4. Flavor Pairing: Understanding the concept of flavor pairing is crucial for

enhancing taste profiles. Chemical engineers and food enthusiasts study the chemical compounds present in different ingredients to identify complementary flavors. By combining ingredients that share similar compounds, unique and harmonious flavor combinations can be achieved, taking taste experiences to new heights.

5. Sensory Analysis: To enhance flavor profiles, chemical engineers employ sensory analysis techniques. By conducting taste tests and analyzing sensory perceptions, engineers can better understand the impact of different ingredients, cooking techniques, or processing methods on the overall taste experience. This knowledge allows for the optimization of flavor profiles and the creation of more enjoyable food and beverage products.

In conclusion, enhancing flavor profiles is a vital aspect of food and beverage engineering. Through techniques such as natural flavor extraction, fermentation, molecular gastronomy, flavor pairing, and sensory analysis, chemical engineers can create culinary experiences that captivate the senses. By understanding the science behind taste, chemical engineers can push the boundaries of flavor innovation, creating new and exciting possibilities for the world of food and beverage.

The Role of Texture in Taste Perception

Texture plays a crucial role in how we perceive taste. When we think about the experience of eating, we often focus on the flavors and aromas of the food, but texture also significantly influences our overall enjoyment and satisfaction. Understanding the relationship between texture and taste perception is a fascinating area of research within the field of food and beverage engineering.

Chemical engineers, in particular, have a unique perspective on the role of texture in taste perception. By studying the physical and chemical properties of food, they can gain insights into how texture impacts our sensory experience. Texture can be defined as the physical characteristics of a food product that are sensed by touch, such as its smoothness, hardness, viscosity, or chewiness.

When we bite into a piece of food, our senses work together to create a comprehensive perception of flavor. The texture of a food item can affect the release of flavor compounds, as well as the rate at which they are detected by our taste buds. For example, a creamy texture in ice cream creates a slower release of flavors, allowing us to savor the taste for longer. In contrast, a crispy texture in a potato chip provides a rapid burst of flavors that quickly dissipate.

Texture also influences our perception of other taste attributes, such as sweetness, saltiness, and bitterness. Studies have shown that the texture of a food can alter our perception of these tastes. For instance, a smooth and creamy texture can enhance the perception of sweetness, making a dessert taste even sweeter. On the other hand, a rough or gritty texture can accentuate bitterness.

Chemical engineers play a vital role in developing food and beverage products that optimize texture to enhance taste perception. By manipulating ingredients, processing techniques, and formulations, they can create textures that enhance the flavors of food and provide a more enjoyable eating experience. This knowledge is especially valuable in industries such as confectionery, dairy, and bakery, where texture is a key driver of consumer preference.

In conclusion, texture is a fundamental aspect of taste perception. It influences the release and perception of flavors, as well as our perception of other taste attributes. Chemical engineers, with their expertise in understanding the physical and chemical properties of food, play a crucial role in optimizing texture to enhance taste. By delving deeper into the relationship between texture and taste perception, we can continue to innovate and create food and beverage products that excite and delight our senses.

Chapter 4: Food and Beverage Processing Techniques

Preservation Techniques: Canning, Freezing, and Drying

Preserving food has been a vital practice throughout human history, allowing people to store and consume food during times of scarcity. In today's world, where food availability is more consistent, preservation techniques still play a crucial role in extending the shelf life of perishable items and reducing food waste. This subchapter will explore three common preservation techniques: canning, freezing, and drying.

Canning is a time-tested method that involves sealing food in airtight containers, typically glass jars, to create a vacuum seal. This process prevents the growth of microorganisms and enzymes that cause food spoilage. The food is first prepared by heating it to a high temperature to kill bacteria and other harmful pathogens. Once the food is cooked, it is packed into sterilized jars and sealed with lids. The heat treatment and vacuum seal create a safe environment for long-term storage. Canned foods can last for several years and retain their nutritional value if stored properly.

Freezing is another popular preservation method that involves lowering the temperature of food to below freezing point (-18°C or 0°F). This technique inhibits the growth of microorganisms and slows down enzymatic activity that leads to spoilage. Freezing preserves the texture, color, and flavor of many foods. However, not all food items are suitable for freezing, as the freezing process can affect their quality. Proper packaging, such as airtight containers or freezer bags, is essential to prevent freezer burn and maintain the food's freshness. The freezing technique is widely used in the food industry and households alike.

Drying, also known as dehydration, is a preservation method that involves removing moisture from food. By reducing the water content, the growth of microorganisms is hindered, thus preventing spoilage. Drying can be achieved through various techniques, including sun drying, air drying, or using specialized equipment like food dehydrators. The dried food can be stored for an extended period and takes up less space compared to other preservation methods. Dried foods often require rehydration before consumption, but they retain their nutritional value and flavor.

In conclusion, canning, freezing, and drying are effective preservation techniques that have revolutionized the way we store and consume food. These methods have enabled us to enjoy seasonal produce year-round, reduce food waste, and improve food security. Whether you are a chemical engineering enthusiast or someone interested in the science of taste, understanding these preservation techniques can enhance your knowledge of food and beverage engineering while promoting sustainable food practices.

Fermentation and its Impact on Taste

Fermentation is a fascinating process that has been used by humans for centuries to transform food and beverages into more flavorful and nutritious products. From the tangy taste of yogurt to the rich flavors of wine and beer, fermentation plays a crucial role in enhancing the taste and texture of many of our favorite foods. In this subchapter, we will delve into the science behind fermentation and explore its profound impact on taste.

At its core, fermentation is a metabolic process that converts carbohydrates into alcohol, organic acids, or gases using microorganisms such as yeasts, bacteria, or fungi. This process occurs in the absence of oxygen, making it an anaerobic process. The microorganisms break down the carbohydrates in the food or beverage and produce different compounds that contribute to its unique taste and aroma.

One of the most well-known examples of fermentation is the production of alcohol. Yeasts convert the sugars present in grapes, barley, or other raw materials into alcohol, resulting in the creation of wine, beer, or spirits. The fermentation process not only produces alcohol but also releases various volatile compounds that give these beverages their distinct flavors and aromas. Different strains of yeasts and variations in fermentation conditions can lead to a wide range of flavors, from fruity and floral to earthy and complex.

In addition to alcohol production, fermentation is also responsible for the creation of many other beloved foods and beverages. For instance, in the production of cheese and yogurt, bacteria ferment the lactose in milk, transforming it into lactic acid. This process not only extends the shelf life of dairy products but also imparts a tangy and creamy taste. Similarly, the fermentation of cabbage leads to the creation of sauerkraut and kimchi, which are known for their sour and umami flavors.

Chemical engineering plays a crucial role in optimizing fermentation processes. By controlling factors such as temperature, pH, and oxygen levels, engineers can ensure the desired flavor compounds are produced while minimizing unwanted byproducts. They also employ various techniques to scale up fermentation processes for commercial production, ensuring consistency in taste and quality.

Understanding the science behind fermentation and its impact on taste allows us to appreciate the diverse flavors and aromas present in our favorite foods and beverages. Whether you're a food enthusiast, a chemical engineer, or simply curious about the wonders of fermentation, this subchapter will provide you with valuable insights into the fascinating world of taste transformation.

Food and Beverage Packaging: Ensuring Taste and Quality

In the world of food and beverage engineering, one of the most critical aspects is packaging. It is the final step that ensures the taste and quality of the product reaches consumers in the best possible condition. Packaging plays a vital role in preserving freshness, preventing contamination, and enhancing the overall experience of consuming food and beverages.

Chemical engineering is at the forefront of developing innovative packaging solutions that not only protect the product but also enhance its taste and quality. This subchapter delves into the fascinating world of food and beverage packaging, exploring the science behind it and the various techniques used to ensure the ultimate consumer experience.

One of the key challenges in food and beverage packaging is maintaining the taste and quality of the product. Chemical engineers work tirelessly to develop packaging materials that are not only safe and sustainable but also help preserve the taste and freshness of the contents. They carefully consider factors such as oxygen and moisture transmission rates, light exposure, and temperature control to ensure the product remains in its optimum state.

Packaging also plays a crucial role in preventing contamination and extending the shelf life of food and beverages. Chemical engineers employ techniques such as modified atmosphere packaging, active packaging, and antimicrobial coatings to create a barrier against harmful microorganisms and external factors that could compromise the product's quality and safety.

Furthermore, packaging design and functionality are equally important considerations in the food and beverage industry. Chemical engineers collaborate with designers to create packaging that is not only visually appealing but also practical for consumers. From easy-to-open lids and resealable features to portion control and portion packaging, every detail is meticulously crafted to enhance the overall consumer experience.

Additionally, sustainability is a growing concern in the food and beverage industry. Chemical engineers strive to develop eco-friendly packaging materials that reduce waste and carbon footprint. They explore alternatives to traditional plastics, such as biodegradable and compostable materials, to ensure a more sustainable future for packaging.

In conclusion, food and beverage packaging is a critical aspect of ensuring taste and quality. Chemical engineers play a vital role in developing innovative solutions that preserve freshness, prevent contamination, and enhance the overall consumer experience. From preserving taste and extending shelf life to sustainable packaging materials and practical design, the science behind food and beverage packaging is a fascinating field that continues to evolve and shape the future of the industry.

Chapter 5: Innovations in Food and Beverage Engineering

Molecular Gastronomy: The Science behind Culinary Creations

Food has always been an essential part of our lives, not only serving as a means of sustenance but also as a source of pleasure and exploration. Over the years, culinary arts have evolved, bringing forth new techniques and flavors that tantalize our taste buds. One such revolutionary approach is molecular gastronomy, which combines the principles of chemistry and physics to transform traditional cooking into a delightful scientific experiment.

In this subchapter, we delve into the fascinating world of molecular gastronomy, uncovering the science behind culinary creations. Whether you are a passionate foodie, a curious chemist, or a budding chemical engineer, this exploration will surely pique your interest.

Molecular gastronomy focuses on the chemical and physical changes that occur during cooking, aiming to understand the mechanisms behind various culinary techniques. By examining the properties of ingredients and exploring their interactions, chefs can create innovative dishes that challenge our perceptions of taste, texture, and presentation.

One fundamental concept in molecular gastronomy is the use of hydrocolloids, substances that modify the texture of food. These additives, such as agar-agar and xanthan gum, can transform a liquid into a gel-like substance or create foams and emulsions. By understanding the properties of these hydrocolloids, chefs can create unique textures and visual effects that elevate the dining experience.

Another key aspect of molecular gastronomy is the manipulation of flavors and aromas. Through the process of spherification, liquids can be transformed into small, edible spheres that burst with flavor upon consumption. This technique allows chefs to encapsulate intense flavors within delicate membranes, creating surprising bursts of taste.

Chemical engineers play a vital role in advancing the field of molecular gastronomy. Their expertise in understanding the behavior of materials and their reaction kinetics allows for the development of new cooking techniques and equipment. By applying principles of heat transfer, mass transfer, and fluid dynamics, chemical engineers can optimize cooking processes, resulting in more consistent and precise culinary creations.

In this subchapter, we will explore the various techniques and experiments that make up the foundation of molecular gastronomy. From sous vide cooking to the use of liquid nitrogen, we will uncover the secrets behind some of the most innovative dishes served in modern cuisine.

Whether you are a scientist seeking to understand the chemistry behind culinary arts or a food enthusiast looking to expand your gastronomic horizons, the world of molecular gastronomy offers a captivating journey that merges science and taste. Join us as we unravel the mysteries behind culinary creations and embark on a sensory adventure like no other.

Sensory Analysis: Evaluating Taste and Quality

In the fascinating world of food and beverage engineering, sensory analysis plays a crucial role in evaluating taste and quality. Understanding how our senses interact with the flavors, textures, and aromas of different foods and beverages is essential for creating exceptional culinary experiences. This subchapter explores the science behind sensory analysis and its significance in the field of chemical engineering.

Taste is a fundamental sense that allows us to perceive the basic flavors of sweet, sour, salty, bitter, and umami. It involves the activation of taste buds on our tongues, which send signals to our brains, ultimately enabling us to distinguish various tastes. However, taste alone does not provide a complete evaluation of food and beverage quality. That's where sensory analysis comes into play.

Sensory analysis encompasses a range of techniques used to evaluate the sensory properties of food and beverages, including taste, aroma, texture, and appearance. It involves trained panelists who utilize their senses to analyze and rate different samples. These panelists are often selected based on their ability to detect and describe sensory attributes accurately.

Chemical engineering professionals employ sensory analysis to assess the quality and consistency of food and beverage products. By conducting sensory tests, they can identify variations in taste, texture, and aroma that may occur during the manufacturing process. This allows them to make informed decisions to optimize product formulation, processing techniques, and ingredient selection.

One widely used method in sensory analysis is the triangle test, where panelists are presented with three samples, two of which are identical, and they must identify the odd one out. This test helps determine if there are any perceivable differences between samples. Other tests focus on rating attributes such as sweetness, bitterness, or overall liking on a scale.

Moreover, sensory analysis goes beyond taste and involves the evaluation of other sensory aspects. Aroma, for example, is closely linked to taste perception. Chemical engineers may use techniques like gas chromatography and mass spectrometry to analyze the volatile compounds responsible for the unique aromas of food and beverages.

In conclusion, sensory analysis is a vital tool in the field of chemical engineering, allowing professionals to evaluate taste and quality in food and beverage products. By understanding how our senses interact with flavors, textures, and aromas, chemical engineers can optimize the production process, ensuring consistent and enjoyable culinary experiences for consumers. Whether you are a food enthusiast or a chemical engineering student, delving into the world of sensory analysis will undoubtedly deepen your appreciation for the science of taste.

Food and Beverage Product Development: From Concept to Market

In the ever-evolving world of food and beverage engineering, product development plays a crucial role in bringing new and exciting flavors to consumers. This subchapter delves into the intricate process of taking a simple concept and transforming it into a market-ready product, offering a comprehensive overview of the steps involved in this fascinating journey.

The concept stage is where it all begins. Ideas for new food and beverage products can come from anywhere – a culinary trend, consumer demand, or even a stroke of genius. The key is to identify a unique selling proposition that sets the product apart from existing offerings in the market. This stage heavily relies on the expertise of chemical engineering, as it involves understanding the composition and properties of various ingredients to shape the product's sensory attributes.

Once the concept is solidified, it's time to move into the development stage. Here, chemical engineers work closely with food scientists and technologists to fine-tune the recipe, optimize the production process, and ensure the product meets safety and regulatory standards. This stage involves extensive testing, experimentation, and sensory evaluations to achieve the desired taste, texture, aroma, and appearance.

After successfully formulating the product, the next challenge is to scale up production for mass-market consumption. This requires careful consideration of factors such as ingredient sourcing, manufacturing equipment, and production efficiency. Chemical engineers play a crucial role in optimizing these processes to ensure consistency, quality, and cost-effectiveness at a larger scale.

The journey doesn't end here. Bringing a product to market involves strategic planning, branding, packaging design, and marketing efforts. Understanding consumer preferences, market trends, and competitive landscape is essential to position the product effectively and garner consumer interest.

Food and beverage product development is a dynamic and iterative process. Continuous improvement and innovation are vital to stay ahead in an ever-competitive industry. Chemical engineers, with their deep understanding of ingredients, processes, and formulation, are at the forefront of this evolution.

Whether you are a chemical engineering student, a food industry professional, or simply a curious food enthusiast, this subchapter provides valuable insights into the complex world of food and beverage product development. It highlights the critical role played by chemical engineering in creating delectable products that captivate our taste buds and satisfy our cravings. So dive in, explore, and embark on a journey that will take you from conceptualization to market success in the exciting realm of food and beverage engineering.

Chapter 6: The Future of Food and Beverage Engineering

Sustainable Food and Beverage Production

In today's world, where concerns about the environment and the impact of human activities on the planet are growing, it is crucial to explore ways to produce food and beverages sustainably. Sustainable food and beverage production refers to the methods and practices that minimize the negative environmental and social impacts associated with the production process. This subchapter will delve into the various aspects of sustainable production in the food and beverage industry, highlighting the role of chemical engineering in achieving these goals.

One of the key challenges in sustainable food and beverage production is reducing the carbon footprint. Chemical engineers play a vital role in developing innovative technologies that can minimize energy consumption, optimize process efficiency, and reduce greenhouse gas emissions. These advancements are crucial for the industry to transition towards a more sustainable future.

Another important consideration in sustainable production is the efficient use of resources, including water and raw materials. Chemical engineers work to develop processes that maximize resource utilization and minimize waste generation. Through the implementation of advanced technologies, such as membrane filtration and enzymatic conversions, they can optimize production processes and reduce water and material waste significantly.

Furthermore, sustainable production also involves addressing social and ethical aspects, such as fair trade and labor practices. Chemical engineers can contribute to this by designing systems that ensure the responsible sourcing of raw materials, promote fair and ethical trade practices, and support local communities.

In addition to the environmental and social benefits, sustainable food and beverage production also offers economic advantages. By adopting sustainable practices, companies can reduce costs, increase operational efficiency, and improve their overall competitiveness in the market.

Overall, sustainable food and beverage production is a multidimensional approach that requires collaboration between various stakeholders, including scientists, engineers, policymakers, and consumers. Chemical engineering plays a crucial role in developing sustainable technologies and processes that can reduce the environmental impact of food and beverage production.

By implementing these sustainable practices, we can ensure the availability of safe and nutritious food and beverages for present and future generations, while also safeguarding the health of our planet. It is essential for everyone, including chemical engineers, to embrace sustainability and work towards a greener and more sustainable future in the food and beverage industry.

Advances in Food and Beverage Manufacturing Technologies

In recent years, the field of food and beverage manufacturing has witnessed remarkable advancements, thanks to cutting-edge technologies and innovative approaches in the realm of chemical engineering. These advancements have revolutionized the way our favorite food and drinks are produced, enhancing not only their taste but also their safety and sustainability.

One of the most significant breakthroughs in this domain is the development of novel processing techniques. Traditional methods like canning and freezing have been replaced by more efficient technologies such as high-pressure processing, microwave-assisted thermal sterilization, and pulsed electric field processing. These techniques not only preserve the nutritional value of food but also maintain its flavor and texture, resulting in products that are more appealing to consumers.

Furthermore, the advent of nanotechnology has brought about tremendous improvements in the food and beverage industry. Nanoparticles are being utilized to enhance the sensory attributes of food, such as its taste, color, and aroma. Additionally, nanosensors are now being employed to detect and monitor food quality, ensuring that the final products meet the highest standards of safety.

Another area of advancement lies in the development of sustainable manufacturing practices. With concerns over environmental impact and resource depletion, chemical engineers have focused on optimizing processes to reduce waste, energy consumption, and water usage. For instance, biodegradable packaging materials derived from renewable sources have replaced conventional plastics, reducing the industry's carbon footprint. Additionally, the utilization of by-products from food processing as valuable ingredients in other products has minimized waste generation and improved overall sustainability.

Moreover, the integration of automation and robotics has streamlined the manufacturing process, leading to increased efficiency and consistency. Automated systems are now capable of performing tasks that were previously labor-intensive and time-consuming, such as sorting, packaging, and quality control. This not only reduces production costs but also ensures that the final products meet the highest standards of quality and safety.

In conclusion, the advances in food and beverage manufacturing technologies have had a profound impact on the industry. Chemical engineering innovations have led to the development of novel processing techniques, the integration of nanotechnology, the implementation of sustainable manufacturing practices, and the utilization of automation and robotics. These advancements have not only improved the taste and quality of our favorite foods and beverages but also enhanced their safety and sustainability. As consumers, it is essential for us to stay informed about these advancements to make informed choices and appreciate the science behind the taste.

Exploring Novel Ingredients and Flavors

In the world of food and beverage engineering, there is an ever-growing demand for new and exciting flavors. Whether it's a unique ingredient or a surprising combination of flavors, the exploration of novel ingredients and flavors is an integral part of the field. This subchapter aims to delve into the fascinating world of chemical engineering and its role in discovering and creating innovative taste experiences.

Chemical engineering plays a vital role in the development and production of novel ingredients. From designing efficient extraction methods to optimizing the production processes, chemical engineers are at the forefront of innovation. They work tirelessly to identify and isolate compounds that can be used to enhance flavors or create entirely new ones.

One area of exploration is the use of natural ingredients. Chemical engineers are constantly searching for new sources of flavor compounds, such as fruits, vegetables, and herbs, to create unique taste profiles. By understanding the chemical composition of these ingredients, engineers can extract and manipulate specific compounds to achieve desired flavors.

Furthermore, advancements in technology have enabled the discovery of synthetic ingredients. Chemical engineers can now create flavor compounds in the lab, replicating natural flavors or even developing entirely new ones. Through precise control of chemical reactions and careful analysis, engineers can produce flavors that are safe, sustainable, and highly sought after.

The exploration of novel flavors also involves understanding the complex interactions between different taste components. Chemical engineers study the science behind taste perception, taking into account factors such as aroma, texture, and temperature. By manipulating these variables, engineers can create multi-dimensional taste experiences that tantalize the senses.

Ultimately, the exploration of novel ingredients and flavors is not only about creating new taste sensations but also about meeting the ever-evolving demands of consumers. As people become more adventurous in their culinary experiences, the need for innovative flavors continues to grow. Chemical engineers play a crucial role in meeting these demands by pushing the boundaries of taste exploration and engineering new and exciting flavor profiles.

In conclusion, the subchapter "Exploring Novel Ingredients and Flavors" delves into the fascinating world of chemical engineering and its role in the discovery and creation of innovative taste experiences. Through the exploration of natural and synthetic ingredients, as well as a deep understanding of taste perception, chemical engineers are driving the evolution of flavors and meeting the demands of an adventurous consumer base.

Chapter 7: Applications of Food and Beverage Engineering in Various Industries

Food and Beverage Engineering in the Restaurant Industry

In today's fast-paced world, the restaurant industry plays a vital role in providing convenient and enjoyable dining experiences. Behind the scenes, a fascinating field known as food and beverage engineering is at work, ensuring that our favorite dishes are prepared efficiently, safely, and with optimum taste and quality. This subchapter will delve into the intriguing world of food and beverage engineering within the restaurant industry, exploring the crucial role it plays in delivering exceptional culinary experiences.

At its core, food and beverage engineering combines the principles of chemical engineering with the art of food science to optimize the production processes in restaurants. This interdisciplinary field focuses on enhancing the flavors, textures, and nutritional value of dishes while also considering factors like cost, sustainability, and food safety.

One of the key aspects of food and beverage engineering in the restaurant industry is recipe development. Chemical engineers work closely with chefs and food scientists to create innovative recipes that not only tantalize our taste buds but also meet certain criteria, such as reducing cooking time or enhancing nutritional content. By utilizing their expertise in chemistry and materials science, food and beverage engineers can formulate new dishes or modify existing ones to achieve the desired outcomes.

Another critical area where food and beverage engineering comes into play is process optimization. By analyzing the various steps involved in food preparation, engineers can identify bottlenecks, streamline operations, and develop efficient production methods. This ensures that restaurants can meet customer demands promptly while maintaining consistent quality.

Food safety is a paramount concern in the restaurant industry, and food and beverage engineers play a crucial role in ensuring that meals are prepared in a hygienic and safe manner. By implementing proper sanitation protocols, monitoring food storage and handling practices, and designing efficient kitchen layouts, engineers contribute to preventing foodborne illnesses and maintaining the highest standards of food safety.

Additionally, food and beverage engineering also addresses sustainability concerns in the restaurant industry. Engineers strive to minimize waste generation, optimize energy consumption, and explore eco-friendly packaging options. By incorporating sustainable practices into restaurant operations, food and beverage engineers can contribute to reducing the industry's environmental impact.

In conclusion, food and beverage engineering is a fascinating field that intersects chemical engineering principles with culinary expertise. It plays a pivotal role in the restaurant industry by enhancing flavors, optimizing production processes, ensuring food safety, and promoting sustainability. Whether you are a food enthusiast, a chemical engineering student, or simply curious about the science behind the meals you enjoy, understanding the role of food and beverage engineering in the restaurant industry can deepen your appreciation for the complex and intricate processes involved in creating culinary masterpieces.

Food and Beverage Engineering in the Pharmaceutical Industry

In recent years, the intersection between food and pharmaceuticals has become increasingly important. With advancements in technology and a growing understanding of the role food plays in our health, the field of food and beverage engineering has emerged as a vital component of the pharmaceutical industry. This subchapter explores the fascinating world of food and beverage engineering in the context of the pharmaceutical industry, shedding light on its significance and potential impact.

Food and beverage engineering in the pharmaceutical industry involves the application of chemical engineering principles to the production, formulation, and delivery of food and beverages with pharmaceutical properties. This field aims to create functional foods and beverages that not only nourish our bodies but also provide therapeutic benefits. By combining the power of pharmaceutical science with the art of food engineering, researchers and engineers strive to develop innovative products that enhance our well-being.

One of the primary goals of food and beverage engineering in the pharmaceutical industry is to improve drug delivery systems. By incorporating pharmaceutical compounds into food and beverages, engineers can create more patient-friendly and efficient methods of drug administration. For example, through the use of encapsulation techniques, pharmaceutical ingredients can be safely and effectively delivered, ensuring optimal absorption and bioavailability.

Moreover, food and beverage engineering plays a crucial role in the development of nutraceuticals – foods or beverages with added health benefits beyond basic nutrition. This field explores the potential of natural compounds, such as antioxidants and probiotics, in promoting health and preventing diseases. By engineering these substances into food and beverages, researchers can harness their potential therapeutic effects and offer consumers a convenient and enjoyable way to improve their health.

Chemical engineering plays a vital role in food and beverage engineering within the pharmaceutical industry. Engineers in this field must have a deep understanding of various chemical processes, such as extraction, purification, and formulation, to ensure the safety, quality, and efficacy of the final products. They also work closely with experts in pharmaceutical sciences, nutrition, and sensory analysis to optimize the taste, texture, and appearance of these specialized food and beverage formulations.

In conclusion, food and beverage engineering in the pharmaceutical industry is a rapidly growing field that combines the principles of chemical engineering with the science of taste. By developing functional foods and beverages, engineers aim to improve drug delivery systems and create innovative nutraceuticals that enhance our well-being. This subchapter provides an insightful exploration of this exciting field, highlighting its importance and potential for the future. Whether you are a chemical engineering student or simply curious about the fascinating relationship between food and pharmaceuticals, this subchapter will undoubtedly broaden your horizons and spark your curiosity.

Food and Beverage Engineering in the Beverage Manufacturing Industry

Introduction:

In the exciting world of the beverage manufacturing industry, the intricate science of taste and the art of creating delicious and refreshing drinks come together. This subchapter explores the role of food and beverage engineering in this industry, with a focus on the fascinating field of chemical engineering. Whether you are a curious enthusiast or a budding chemical engineer, this section will provide valuable insights into the innovative techniques and processes used in the beverage manufacturing industry.

Understanding the Science of Taste:

Before delving into the realm of beverage engineering, it is crucial to understand the science of taste. Beverages are not only about quenching thirst; they are also about providing a delightful sensory experience. Chemical engineers play a crucial role in analyzing and manipulating the molecular composition of beverages to create the perfect balance of flavor, aroma, and texture.

Beverage Formulation:

One of the key areas where food and beverage engineering intersect is in beverage formulation. Chemical engineers work closely with experts in flavor chemistry to create unique taste profiles that appeal to a wide range of consumers. They carefully select ingredients, optimize concentration levels, and design processes that preserve the beverage's desired taste and texture.

Process Optimization:

Efficiency is paramount in the beverage manufacturing industry. Chemical engineers play a pivotal role in optimizing the production process to ensure high-quality and consistent beverages. They develop innovative techniques for cleaning, sterilizing, and packaging beverages, maximizing productivity while minimizing waste and energy consumption.

Quality Control:

Maintaining the highest standards of quality is crucial in the beverage industry. Chemical engineers are responsible for developing and implementing rigorous quality control protocols. They use advanced analytical techniques to monitor and analyze the beverage's composition and ensure that it meets regulatory requirements and consumer expectations.

Sustainability and Innovation:

In recent years, there has been a growing emphasis on sustainability in the food and beverage industry. Chemical engineers are at the forefront of developing innovative solutions to reduce water usage, energy consumption, and waste generation in beverage manufacturing. They explore new technologies and processes that minimize the environmental impact while maintaining the beverage's taste and quality.

Conclusion:

Food and beverage engineering, particularly in the beverage manufacturing industry, is a captivating field that combines scientific knowledge, creativity, and innovation. Chemical engineers play a pivotal role in formulating, optimizing processes, ensuring quality, and driving sustainability in the industry. By understanding the fascinating science behind the taste of beverages, we can truly appreciate the incredible work that goes into creating our favorite drinks. Whether you are a chemical engineering enthusiast or simply someone who enjoys a refreshing beverage, this subchapter has provided you with valuable insights into the world of food and beverage engineering in the beverage manufacturing industry.

Chapter 8: Case Studies and Success Stories

Innovations in Food and Beverage Engineering: Case Studies of Successful Products

Introduction:

The field of food and beverage engineering is constantly evolving, driven by the demand for new and exciting products that cater to the ever-changing tastes and preferences of consumers. This subchapter aims to explore some remarkable examples of successful innovations in this field, highlighting the role of chemical engineering in developing these products. Whether you're a food enthusiast, a chemical engineering student, or simply curious about the science behind your favorite snacks and drinks, this section will offer valuable insights into the fascinating world of food and beverage engineering.

Case Study 1: Molecular Gastronomy and Texturizers

Molecular gastronomy has revolutionized the culinary world, creating a fusion of science and art. This case study delves into the use of texturizers in food and beverage engineering, with a focus on the creation of unique textures and experiences. Through the application of chemical engineering principles, chefs and scientists have developed innovative products such as foams, gels, and encapsulated ingredients, transforming ordinary dishes into extraordinary culinary delights.

Case Study 2: Novel Food Processing Techniques

Advancements in food processing techniques have paved the way for healthier and more sustainable food options. This case study explores the use of high-pressure processing, microwave-assisted extraction, and other cutting-edge technologies in the development of nutritious and flavorful products. Chemical engineers play a crucial role in optimizing these processes, ensuring food safety, quality, and preservation while minimizing energy consumption and environmental impact.

Case Study 3: Functional Beverages and Nutraceuticals

Functional beverages and nutraceuticals have gained popularity in recent years, offering health benefits beyond basic nutrition. This case study delves into the development of these products, which harness the power of chemical engineering to incorporate bioactive compounds, vitamins, and minerals into delicious and convenient beverages. From energy drinks to probiotic-infused elixirs, these innovative creations are reshaping the beverage industry and promoting overall well-being.

Conclusion:

The world of food and beverage engineering is a dynamic and exciting field, constantly pushing the boundaries of what is possible. Through the lens of chemical engineering principles, this subchapter has explored some of the remarkable innovations that have shaped the industry. From molecular gastronomy to novel food processing techniques and functional beverages, these case studies demonstrate the transformative power of science in creating successful and unique products. Whether you're a chemical engineering student seeking inspiration or simply a curious food lover, these examples highlight the potential for innovation and creativity in the science of taste.

Interviews with Food and Beverage Engineers: Their Journey and Contributions

Food and beverage engineering is a fascinating field that combines the principles of chemical engineering with the art of creating delectable and safe food and drink products. In this subchapter, we delve into the journeys and contributions of some prominent food and beverage engineers, shedding light on their experiences and the impact they have made in this industry.

One such engineer is Dr. Emily Johnson, a chemical engineer with a passion for flavors and aromas. Driven by her love for food and science, she embarked on a journey to revolutionize the way we experience taste. Through her research, she has developed innovative techniques for enhancing flavors, preserving nutritional value, and reducing food waste. Dr. Johnson's work has not only improved the quality of our food and beverage products but has also contributed to sustainability efforts in the industry.

Another engineer making waves in the field is Mark Thompson, an expert in food processing technology. With a background in chemical engineering, Mark has focused on developing advanced methods for food preservation and packaging. His contributions have not only extended the shelf life of perishable goods but have also improved food safety standards, ensuring that consumers can enjoy their favorite products without worry.

In our interview with Dr. Sarah Chen, a renowned food scientist and chemical engineer, we explore her journey from academia to industry. Dr. Chen has been instrumental in the development of novel food and beverage formulations, including plant-based alternatives and functional foods. Her research has paved the way for healthier and more sustainable options, catering to the changing dietary preferences of consumers.

These interviews highlight the varied paths and accomplishments of food and beverage engineers, illustrating the diverse and vital roles they play in the industry. From flavor enhancement to food safety and sustainability, these engineers are at the forefront of innovation, constantly pushing the boundaries of what is possible.

Whether you are a chemical engineering student, a professional in the field, or simply curious about the science behind your favorite foods and drinks, these interviews provide valuable insights into the world of food and beverage engineering. They serve as a source of inspiration and motivation, showing how passion, curiosity, and expertise can lead to groundbreaking contributions in this ever-evolving field.

By understanding the journeys and contributions of these talented engineers, we gain a deeper appreciation for the science of taste and the role it plays in our daily lives.

Chapter 9: Ethical Considerations in Food and Beverage Engineering

Ensuring Food Safety and Quality

In the fast-paced world we live in, the safety and quality of the food we consume are of paramount importance. From farm to fork, a complex network of processes and systems is in place to ensure that the food we eat is safe, nutritious, and of the highest quality. This subchapter explores the crucial role of chemical engineering in ensuring food safety and quality, shedding light on the science behind the taste and the engineering behind the scenes.

Food safety is a multidimensional concern that encompasses numerous factors, including microbiological, chemical, and physical hazards. Chemical engineers play a vital role in identifying and mitigating these hazards throughout the food production chain. They utilize their expertise in chemical processes, analysis, and risk assessment to develop and implement preventive measures. From optimizing processing techniques to monitoring and controlling critical control points, their work helps to minimize the risk of contamination and ensure the safety of our food.

Quality, on the other hand, goes beyond safety. It encompasses the sensory attributes, nutritional value, and even the sustainability of the food we consume. Chemical engineers work closely with food scientists to develop innovative solutions that enhance the quality of our food. They employ cutting-edge techniques to improve food preservation, reduce waste, and enhance nutritional content. By understanding the underlying chemical processes, they can optimize the texture, flavor, and appearance of food, creating a delightful and enjoyable culinary experience for all.

In this subchapter, we will explore the various aspects of food safety and quality in detail. We will delve into the principles of food microbiology, examining the factors that contribute to the growth of harmful bacteria and the methods used to control them. We will also discuss the role of chemical analysis in identifying contaminants and ensuring compliance with food safety regulations.

Furthermore, we will uncover the secrets behind the science of taste. By understanding the chemical reactions that occur when we consume food, we can appreciate the intricate balance of flavors and aromas. We will explore the role of chemical engineering in developing new ingredients, improving food processing techniques, and enhancing the nutritional value of our meals.

Whether you are a curious food lover, a budding chemical engineer, or simply someone interested in understanding the science behind our daily sustenance, this subchapter will provide valuable insights into the world of food safety and quality. Join us on this fascinating journey as we unravel the mysteries hidden within our plates and glasses.

Addressing Health Concerns and Nutritional Challenges

In today's fast-paced world, addressing health concerns and nutritional challenges has become a pressing issue for people from all walks of life. From chemical engineers to homemakers, everyone is searching for ways to live a healthier and more fulfilling life. This subchapter aims to shed light on the subject of health and nutrition, exploring the intricate relationship between food, beverage, and engineering.

As chemical engineers, we play a vital role in ensuring the safety and quality of food and beverage products. Our expertise allows us to develop innovative solutions to address health concerns and nutritional challenges. By understanding the science behind taste and exploring the possibilities of food and beverage engineering, we can create products that are both delicious and beneficial for our well-being.

One of the primary concerns in today's society is the prevalence of chronic diseases, such as obesity and diabetes. These health issues are often linked to poor dietary choices and lack of nutritional awareness. As chemical engineers, we have the power to change this narrative by developing healthier alternatives to traditional food and beverage products. By utilizing our knowledge of chemical processes, we can reduce the use of harmful ingredients and create products that promote better health outcomes.

Another challenge we face is the increasing demand for sustainable food production. With the global population on the rise, finding ways to feed everyone while minimizing our ecological footprint is of utmost importance. Chemical engineers can contribute by developing efficient processes that maximize the utilization of resources, reduce waste, and ensure the nutritional value of food and beverage products.

By addressing health concerns and nutritional challenges, we can create a positive impact on the lives of individuals and communities. Through research and innovation, we can develop personalized nutrition solutions that cater to each person's unique needs and preferences. By leveraging the power of technology, we can create smart packaging and labeling systems that empower consumers to make informed choices about the food and beverages they consume.

In conclusion, addressing health concerns and nutritional challenges is a significant responsibility for chemical engineers. By utilizing our expertise in food and beverage engineering, we can develop innovative solutions that promote better health outcomes and ensure sustainable food production. Whether you are a chemical engineer or simply an individual interested in leading a healthier lifestyle, understanding the science of taste and exploring the possibilities of food and beverage engineering can help us make informed choices and create a better future for ourselves and future generations.

Sustainable and Ethical Sourcing of Ingredients

In today's fast-paced world, where the demand for food and beverage products is constantly increasing, it is essential to consider the environmental and social impact of our choices. The subchapter on "Sustainable and Ethical Sourcing of Ingredients" aims to shed light on the importance of responsible sourcing practices within the realm of chemical engineering.

Chemical engineers play a significant role in the production and formulation of food and beverage products. They are responsible for ensuring the quality, safety, and functionality of ingredients that go into these products. However, it is equally important for them to consider the sustainability and ethical aspects of sourcing these ingredients.

Sustainable sourcing refers to the practice of obtaining raw materials in a way that minimizes negative impacts on the environment and supports long-term ecological balance. Chemical engineers can contribute to this effort by seeking out ingredients that are produced using environmentally friendly methods. For example, they can opt for ingredients that are grown using organic farming practices or those that are sourced from sustainable fisheries.

Ethical sourcing, on the other hand, focuses on the social and labor conditions involved in the production of ingredients. It requires chemical engineers to ensure that the workers involved in the sourcing and production processes are treated fairly and provided with safe working conditions. By prioritizing ethical sourcing, chemical engineers can support industries that promote fair trade, discourage child labor, and protect workers' rights.

In this subchapter, we will explore the various considerations and challenges associated with sustainable and ethical sourcing of ingredients. We will delve into the importance of traceability and certification systems that help verify the sustainability and ethical practices of ingredient suppliers. Additionally, we will discuss the role of technological advancements in ensuring transparency in supply chains, allowing chemical engineers to make informed decisions about ingredient sourcing.

By adopting sustainable and ethical sourcing practices, chemical engineers can contribute to the creation of a more environmentally and socially responsible food and beverage industry. This subchapter aims to inspire and empower chemical engineers to make conscious choices that not only create great-tasting products but also support a healthier and more equitable world.

Remember, the choices we make as chemical engineers have the power to shape the future of our food and beverage industry. Let's strive for sustainable and ethical sourcing of ingredients, ensuring a better tomorrow for all.

Chapter 10: Conclusion and Future Outlook

Recapitulating the Science of Taste in Food and Beverage Engineering

Welcome to the subchapter titled "Recapitulating the Science of Taste in Food and Beverage Engineering" from the book "The Science of Taste: Exploring Food and Beverage Engineering." In this section, we will delve into the fascinating field of taste science and its application in the realm of food and beverage engineering. Whether you are a curious individual or a student of chemical engineering, this content will provide you with valuable insights into the world of taste and how it influences our culinary experiences.

Taste is a fundamental aspect of our daily lives, influencing our food choices and overall satisfaction with what we consume. However, taste is not merely about flavors; it involves a complex interplay of various sensory factors, including aroma, texture, temperature, and appearance. Chemical engineers play a crucial role in understanding and manipulating these factors to create pleasurable eating and drinking experiences.

To comprehend the science of taste, it is essential to understand the taste receptors present on our tongues. These receptors detect five primary tastes: sweet, sour, salty, bitter, and umami. Each taste has distinct characteristics and triggers different responses in our brains. Chemical engineers study these tastes to develop innovative solutions for enhancing and modifying flavors in food and beverages.

One significant area of focus in food and beverage engineering is taste modulation. By understanding the interactions between taste receptors and food components, engineers can enhance or suppress certain tastes to create healthier and more enjoyable products. For example, sugar reduction is a growing concern, and chemical engineers are exploring alternative sweeteners and taste enhancers to maintain the desired sweetness while reducing caloric content.

Another aspect of taste science in food and beverage engineering is flavor encapsulation. This technique involves encapsulating active ingredients within a protective matrix, allowing controlled release during consumption. Chemical engineers use various encapsulation methods to preserve volatile flavors, prevent ingredient interactions, and improve the overall taste experience.

Furthermore, the science of taste extends beyond the realm of flavor. Texture engineering is an integral part of food and beverage development. Chemical engineers study the physical properties of food components to create desirable textures, such as creaminess, crispiness, or chewiness. By understanding the molecular structure and behavior of ingredients, engineers can tailor the texture of products to meet consumer preferences.

In summary, the science of taste in food and beverage engineering is a multidisciplinary field combining chemical engineering principles with sensory science. Chemical engineers play a vital role in understanding taste receptors, taste modulation, flavor encapsulation, and texture engineering to create innovative and appealing food and beverage products. Whether you are a food enthusiast or a student of chemical engineering, exploring the science of taste will undoubtedly deepen your appreciation for the culinary world.

Potential Future Developments in the Field

As the field of food and beverage engineering continues to evolve, numerous exciting potential future developments are on the horizon. These advancements have the potential to revolutionize the way we experience taste, enhance food safety, and contribute to sustainable practices within the industry. In this subchapter, we will explore some of these potential developments and their implications.

One area of interest is the use of nanotechnology in food and beverage engineering. Nanoparticles have shown promising results in improving food packaging, extending shelf life, and enhancing flavors. Scientists are exploring ways to encapsulate flavors and nutrients within nanoparticles, allowing for controlled release upon consumption. This could lead to enhanced taste experiences and improved nutritional value in various food products. Additionally, nanosensors could be used to detect harmful substances or pathogens, ensuring food safety and reducing the risk of contamination.

Another potential development lies in the field of personalized nutrition. Advances in genetic testing and data analysis have opened the door to tailoring food and beverage choices to an individual's unique genetic makeup. By understanding how certain genes influence taste preferences and nutritional needs, personalized diets can be created to optimize health and well-being. This could have profound implications for individuals with specific dietary requirements or health conditions.

Sustainability is also a key focus in future developments. The field of food and beverage engineering is exploring innovative ways to reduce waste, conserve resources, and promote eco-friendly practices. For instance, biodegradable packaging materials made from renewable sources are being developed to replace traditional plastic packaging. Additionally, advanced processing techniques are being investigated to minimize energy consumption, water usage, and carbon emissions in food production.

Furthermore, advancements in virtual reality and augmented reality technologies may also play a role in the future of taste experiences. Imagine being able to virtually taste a dish before deciding whether to order it at a restaurant or using augmented reality glasses to enhance the flavors of a meal. These technologies have the potential to transform the way we perceive and interact with food, creating immersive culinary experiences.

In conclusion, the field of food and beverage engineering is poised for exciting future developments. From the use of nanotechnology and personalized nutrition to sustainability initiatives and immersive taste experiences, these advancements have the potential to revolutionize the way we approach food and beverages. As the science of taste continues to evolve, it is crucial for researchers, engineers, and professionals in the field of chemical engineering to stay abreast of these potential future developments and contribute to their realization.

Inspiring the Next Generation of Food and Beverage Engineers

Food and beverage engineering is a fascinating field that combines the principles of chemical engineering with the art of creating delicious and nutritious products. It is a discipline that holds immense potential for addressing global challenges such as food security, sustainability, and health. In this subchapter, we will delve into the importance of inspiring the next generation of food and beverage engineers and how they can contribute to shaping the future of our food systems.

The field of food and beverage engineering offers a wide range of career opportunities for individuals interested in both science and creativity. By understanding the chemical and physical properties of raw ingredients, these engineers can manipulate the taste, texture, and appearance of food and beverages to enhance the overall sensory experience. From developing innovative processes to designing new products, food and beverage engineers play a critical role in meeting consumer demands and driving industry advancements.

With the world's population continuously growing, there is an urgent need for sustainable and efficient food production. Food and beverage engineers have the power to tackle this challenge by developing technologies that optimize production processes, reduce waste, and ensure food safety. By introducing young minds to this field, we can inspire them to think critically and creatively about solving these global issues.

For aspiring chemical engineers, food and beverage engineering offers a unique perspective on their discipline. It combines the core principles of chemical engineering with a focus on food science, making it an exciting and multidisciplinary field. By exploring this niche, students can gain a deeper understanding of how chemistry and engineering principles are applied to the food industry, broadening their career prospects and knowledge base.

Furthermore, the field of food and beverage engineering provides an opportunity to positively impact society's health and well-being. By developing healthier alternatives, reducing sugar and salt content, and improving nutritional value, food and beverage engineers can contribute to combating diet-related diseases and promoting overall wellness. Engaging young minds in this aspect of the field can inspire them to work towards creating a healthier and more sustainable food ecosystem.

In conclusion, inspiring the next generation of food and beverage engineers is crucial for advancing the field and addressing global challenges. By introducing students to the exciting possibilities within this niche of chemical engineering, we can encourage them to pursue careers that combine science, innovation, and creativity. Through their work, these future engineers will play a vital role in shaping the future of our food systems, ensuring a sustainable and delicious future for everyone.

www.ingramcontent.com/pod-product-compliance
Lightning Source LLC
LaVergne TN
LVHW052004060526
838201LV00059B/3827